UNDERSTANDING
CHILDREN SPELLING

UNDERSTANDING CHILDREN SPELLING

Jennifer E Barr

Scottish Council for Research in Education

SCRE Publication 90

ISBN 0 947833 12 9

Printed and bound in Great Britain for the Scottish Council for Research in Education, 15 St John Street, Edinburgh EH8 8JR, by Macdonald Printers (Edinburgh) Limited, Edgefield Road, Loanhead, Midlothian.

CONTENTS

| | | *Page* |
| PREFACE | | vii |

SECTION ONE — UNDERSTANDING SPELLING — 1
Introduction — 1
Understanding the Task of Spelling — 2
Summary — 6

SECTION TWO — RELATING SPELLING TO OTHER LANGUAGE SKILLS — 8
Spelling, Speaking and Listening — 8
Spelling and Handwriting — 8
Spelling and Reading — 9
Spelling and Writing — 12
Summary — 14

SECTION THREE — UNDERSTANDING SPELLING IN THE SPELLING LESSON AND IN FLUENT WRITING — 16
Learning from the Spelling Lesson — 16
Generalising from the Spelling Lesson — 17
Case Study: The Spelling Lesson and Speed Writing — 18
Summary: Influences on Spelling in Writing — 28

SECTION FOUR — UNDERSTANDING SPELLING IN DIFFERENT KINDS OF WRITING — 30
Introduction — 30
Making Comparisons across Different Types of Writing — 32
Appreciating the Demands of Different Writing Tasks — 34
Dictation — 34
Copying — 34
Short Answer Tasks and the Problems of Specialised Vocabulary — 35
Summary — 38

SECTION FIVE HELPING CHILDREN BECOME BETTER
          SPELLERS   39
          Encouraging Pupil Autonomy   39
          Responding to Children's Writing   40
          Pinpointing Vocabulary Needs   42
          Addressing Spelling in the Primary School   43
          Addressing Spelling in the Secondary School 45
          Summary and Conclusions   47

REFERENCES   48

BIBLIOGRAPHY   50

LIST OF FIGURES

1 An Example of David's Writing in School, taken from a first year geography examination script.

2 Three Speed Writing Stories by David, written (a) at the beginning, (b) in the middle and (c) at the end of the study.

3 Various Attempts at Spelling the Term 'Magnification', taken from the science worksheet of an eleven year old boy.

4 Writing by Paul, Aged Seven, reproduced as in the original.

PREFACE

There is a tightrope to be walked. Concern for spelling is not exclusively the domain of particular primary teachers nor, indeed, of specific teachers in secondary schools. It is rightly the province of *all* teachers who are involved in directing and responding to children's writing, however routine or demanding the learning task and whatever the type and purpose of the writing. That is on the one hand. On the other hand, we must take care as teachers to keep spelling in its place. Too much of the wrong kind of attention to spelling can inhibit children when they are writing: they become less free to focus on what it is they want to say, and they learn caution in selecting vocabulary, producing writing which tends to be bland and colourless. It is not only in writing that such inhibitions can apply:

> 'They taste delicious', said Elizabeth. (I can't bear this: meal after meal of trying to make things right—of keeping them dull so that they won't go wrong).
>
> Howard (1971), p 32.

This booklet is designed to offer help to teachers and parents who have encountered the dilemma. If we can fathom the spelling task and appreciate how it is that mature writers acquire and use their skill, then we will be in a stronger position to respond sensitively and appropriately to the attempts of children as they use spelling in their day to day writing. Understanding how different individuals tackle learning to spell is useful not just for those who are working with young children but also in guiding older, failing spellers. Accurate spelling is not merely a case of good manners, it is the result of good habits and is grounded in an interest in words and a care with how they are produced.

Three of the five sections in the booklet (Sections 1, 2 and 5) offer a general introduction to guide our understanding of the process of children spelling. I am grateful to many of the writers who have addressed these issues for teachers for a number of ideas which are touched on in these sections. (Full details are given in the bibliography).

There is now a good deal of excellent help available to teachers who wish to understand how children learn to spell isolated words.

However, there is less in the literature about how children go about *using* these words when they are involved in the actual process of writing. This has been the main focus of several studies which I have conducted in recent years*, and while I am not attempting to report research in this booklet, I do draw on lessons from these investigations in discussing how specific features of the writing task can influence both children's choice of words and the accuracy of the spelling (Sections 3 and 4).

Taken together, therefore, the booklet offers practical insights from recent, original research, set within a more general introduction to the topic. Examples come from my own work with children in both primary and secondary schools, and the implications are developed for teachers in both these sectors.

I am grateful to Professor Margaret Clark who was my supervisor and colleague at the time when the ideas were developing, and to Professor Ted Glynn who provided much of the stimulus for debate. My brother Peter typed the script. A major benefit of the written medium is that it allows you to work on clarifying your message, and I am indebted to Mr John Powell and his staff at SCRE for their help in steering the document swiftly through various stages of drafting. Finally, I would like to acknowledge the teachers and pupils in the schools where I work, whose joint insistence that theory must at all times be closely tied to practice provides a continuing focus which it is hard to ignore.

* These studies, together with fuller reviews of work in spelling and writing, are reported in a PhD thesis entitled *Spelling in the Context of Writing for a Purpose* (Barr, 1983).

SECTION ONE

UNDERSTANDING SPELLING

Introduction

'It is a pity that Claucer, who had geneyus, was so
unedicated. He's the wuss speller I know of.'

Artemus Ward (1867), p 24.

Whether we like it or not, we make judgements about people on
the basis of how they spell. Indeed, at times we can find it hard to
see beyond the spelling in a piece of writing to what the writer is
saying. (If you doubt this, ask how often 'Watch your spelling' is the
only comment written by a teacher at the foot of a child's script,
or how frequently job applicants are rejected without an interview
on the basis of the impression created by their spelling and
handwriting on the application form.) Where the errors can be
'read', as in the above quotation, the recipient can still manage to
work out the writer's meaning. Where errors bear little resemblance
to the intended words (eg, 'rechig' for 'require'; 'grarall' for'
gradually') then the poor spelling itself can become a genuine
barrier to communication.

How to help children become competent spellers is a question
which has exercised parents and teachers for over a century. Do
children 'catch' spelling in the course of reading and writing, or
does the skill need to be taught specifically? Which teaching
approaches are most effective, how should words be selected for
study, and how frequently should specific types of spelling lessons
take place? More crucially, how can spelling instruction be so woven
into the general fabric of language work that children can make full
use of their expanding spelling knowledge when they are involved
in day to day writing, and when they find themselves faced with new
writing situations and new vocabulary? To what extent might there
be differences between children in their general approach to
spelling, and how might a teacher's handling of the task vary with
the age, general language level and preferred learning style
(including, where relevant, specific learning difficulty) of individual
pupils? Is there ever a case for saying that spelling should be
ignored? Could too much attention to spelling be harmful?

1

These are just some of the questions which have been explored in the literature. A selected list of useful books for teachers can be found in the bibliography at the end of the booklet. Two of the clearest introductions, both readily obtainable in Britain, are a booklet by Torbe (1978) and the *Catchwords Manual* by Peters and Cripps (1983). I shall not attempt to cover the same ground here: the purpose of this opening chapter is simply to provide a backcloth (both for teachers who are already familiar with much that is known about skill in spelling, and for those for whom such detail is new) and to set the scene for a deeper analysis in subsequent chapters of spelling as it occurs in genuine, purposeful writing.

Understanding the Task of Spelling

The most crucial point to grasp is that providing the correct spelling of a word is not just a simple, routine task involving the use of rote memory, but a complex psycholinguistic activity in which the writer is constantly drawing on vocabulary knowledge to form and test hypotheses about how words are structured in English. Yes, the goal for all writers is to be able to spell *quickly* and *correctly* with a minimum of attention to the process, but this is a stage reached by the mature user of language. It is not the task which becomes simple, but the writer who becomes skilled at processing complex information simultaneously at several levels, thereby freeing attention for more important jobs in writing, such as planning ahead or selecting appropriate form and style of expression.

The problem for most of us is that we have forgotten just how complex the process of developing confidence and mastery in spelling can be. I find that most adults who tell me they are bad spellers will actually spell correctly about 98% of what they write. In addition, they can indicate which words are likely to contain errors, even if they cannot correct them spontaneously. This is the behaviour of a competent speller! Poor spellers or struggling learners are never certain when a word might contain an error, and this means they can neither be sure when they are wrong nor confident when they are right. How frequently do we tell pupils that their spelling is careless! Yet the problem with poor spellers is often that they are being too *careful*, applying spelling rules to new words with elaborate precision in the desperate hope that they may somehow hit on the solution to our illogical and apparently arbitrarily-determined system of written language.

Spelling rules are little help until you already know the answers and can see the patterns. Largely, this is because English orthography is complex, influenced by several different language systems, and still under process of development and reconstruction by its users. There is no straight one-to-one correspondence between sound and written symbol in English: the letter 'a' is pronounced differently when it occurs in 'wall' and 'wag', for example, and variations of the sound [shun] can be written in English words as 'tion' (station), 'shion' (cushion), 'sion' (expansion), 'sian' (Asian) 'cion' (suspicion), 'cian' (magician) and 'cean' (ocean). This is not to say, however, that there is no consistent pattern behind decisions about word structure. There may not be a clear one-to-one correspondence, but English spelling is predictable in terms of general probabilities: in the above example, 85% of words containing the sound [shun] are represented by the letter pattern 'tion'. What you find is that the first attempt of the learner who is developing a grasp of English word structure will often be to use 'tion' (eg, 'occation' for 'occasion') and that, if told this is wrong, the learner will proceed to select the next option in the line of probabilities. By contrast, the struggling speller will not have developed the same feel for what is permissible and likely and may offer an attempt such as 'ockayshun'. It is the predictability within the English writing system which makes it possible for writers to apply spelling knowledge to new words, and to be developing a general feel for the language as specific words are studied and mastered. I should stress that it is not necessary that children should be able to articulate these principles about probabilities, just as young infants do not have to be able to describe grammatical principles as they develop a feel for grammatical usage in speech. It is enough that the principles can be applied when they are needed.

We, who are highly familiar with textual language and accustomed to handling it with some ease, have probably forgotten how distinct the written system is from speech and how dependent it can be on conventions, many of them arbitrary. We need to peel back the layers to begin to understand and appreciate some of the complexity. Young children can help us, for as they take their first struggling attempts to use the written medium to communicate real messages, they are involved in the reverse process—building up the layers piece by piece. Clearest lessons come from the children who have not yet learned to read, who have no prior knowledge of the system. Thus Paul, aged five, wrote 'RUDF' (Are you deaf?) when he found that he could not attract his mother's attention by talking*. The example is intriguing. Paul selects only the most crucial information to be recorded (consonants but not vowels; some of the letters operating through their names and some through their sound), and he has not yet grasped that the steady stream of sound which he hears in speech is in fact a sequence of individual words, signalled in writing by the insertion of spaces between discrete items. These are lessons which he will pick up in due course, once he has established a working system and once he is ready for such refinements. I find it interesting to speculate that Paul's approach may have a developmental significance, since similar features are evident in the historical progression of certain classical languages: vowels were not included in the written script for the first thousand years of Hebrew writing (if the pronunciation was forgotten, new vowels had to be added eg, 'Yahweh' became 'Jehovah'); in Greek script, spaces were first inserted between words around 8th Century AD.

Although initially Paul's grasp of sound-symbol correspondence in written English was at a level that was functional and rudimentary, gradually he came to appreciate more of the rich information which words can carry (information about the sound, meaning, and historical development of the word) and his attempted spellings came to reflect this understanding and his developing feel for the probabilities of particular sounds being represented in particular ways. So when he was five he wrote 'drakthens' for 'directions'; when seven, 'direkshons'; when eight years two months, 'directions'. Only when eight years seven months, however, did he write 'directions' and know with confidence that he was correct.

If this description only touches upon some of the rich information which young spellers are beginning to acquire, understanding how fluent spellers apply their even more detailed knowledge when they approach new words is a far more complex matter. Think yourself of what you do when you hear a new name (eg 'Sivers' or 'Mathieson'). The name may be repeated to you several times, yet you may still be diffident about pronouncing it. This is because you have not yet isolated it from a number of possibilities ('Sives' and 'Sivess' are bona fide surnames which, given certain pronunciations, can sound similar to 'Sivers'). If you were to receive feedback on your pronunciation attempts or were to

---

* This interesting case study is described in full by Paul's mother in Bissex (1980), and there are similar lessons from children from downtown Mexico in Ferreiro and Teberosky (1983). See also Payton (1984).

see the name written down, this first source of ambiguity would be removed—now you would know which name you are meant to be learning. However, even when you have ascertained the correct sound of the name, you may not yet have immediate access to the correct spelling. If we take the example of 'Mathieson', the telephone book for my local area identifies six possible renderings ('Matheson', 'Mathewson', 'Mathieson', 'Mathison', 'Mattewson', 'Matthewson') and there may be even more. Knowing the correct sound of the word reduces some of the ambiguity, and having at your fingertips information about possible letter combinations in English (for example, the spelling is unlikely to be 'Maathesonn') reduces it some more, but the furthest you can get with this analysis is a list of possible options. Choosing between the options will be settled by studying the visual form of the word, and the more aware you are of likely sources of confusion, the more efficient you can be in directing your attention. In this instance, noting that there is a single 't', and that the middle syllable is written 'thie' will distinguish this spelling from the others. As Margaret Peters stresses, providing accurate spelling is at heart a visual-motor skill, and children learn most efficiently when they are trained to be able to study and memorise the visual form of a word*. However, understanding a range of other aspects of word structure can also help in focussing attention, thereby narrowing the search for the answer.

It is not just information about word shape or appreciating the regularity/irregularity of sound-symbol relations that can be useful to the speller. Understanding how words are constructed can also be of value. Knowing that 'magician' is derived from the root 'magic' and is related to it in meaning helps to solve that particular puzzle. For more advanced students, understanding something of the various influences on English from other languages (eg Latin, Anglo-Saxon) can help the learner detect consistent patterns, particularly when applying prefixes and suffixes. Go no further for examples than back through the last sentence: eg ad- (L), under- (A.S.), con- (L), -ing (A.S.), -ly (A.S.). Some recent research studies have also indicated that knowing the meaning of a word can aid spelling accuracy. Certainly, we all know that when children have something genuine to write about and a clearly identified audience to be writing for, the quality of their spelling improves (a point to which I still return repeatedly throughout this booklet). Familiarity with the words which they are trying to spell is essential if the task

* Peters (1983).

5

of spelling is to have any meaning and purpose for children, and in this context it is perhaps significant that the examples of bizarre spelling which I quoted on page 1 ('rechig' and 'grarall') were drawn, not from children's fluent writing, but from a dictated spelling test. The girl who writes 'speacist' for 'species' on a science worksheet might not strictly be making a spelling error: she may not really be sure what the word is that she is meant to be writing. Both word length and how frequently the word is used in general writing can also have a bearing on the ease with which the spelling is learned.

Summary

In this opening section, I have outlined some of the complex processing which takes place as we learn to spell words in English and as we use this knowledge when tackling new and unfamiliar vocabulary. The English system of representing words in writing is rich in the information which it carries—there can be hints as to how the word sounds, what it means, how it is derived, the grammatical function which it serves—and fluent language users can draw on various aspects of this information as they generate and test individual spellings. It follows that when a mistake is made it is rarely arbitrary; instead it will signal the particular approach which the writer has adopted. Understanding this and helping the writer to correct distortions of emphasis (for example, too much attention to the sound pattern of the word and too little attention to the visual shape) is important in helping writers refine their approach and in reducing the likelihood of future errors. Clearly, there will be differences in the quality of the attempts of beginning spellers and of more fluent writers, and the amount of specific attention which learners have to pay to the task will gradually reduce as they increase both their vocabulary knowledge and their understanding of and feel for word structure. Fluent spellers have developed a wide range of strategies which they can adopt when spelling, and their greatest strength is a flexibility in being able to select the most appropriate approach in any given instance. Practical implications of this analysis are detailed, both for primary and secondary school children and for competent and struggling spellers, in the final section of the booklet.

One difficulty with looking at spelling in this way is that it could be taken to imply that spelling can be examined in isolation from other literacy skills. Yet even in this brief discussion we have seen that knowledge of vocabulary is an important adjunct to spelling, as indeed are an appreciation of grammar, word function, etymology, and meaning. Clear and fluent handwriting is also important. On a more fundamental level, unless spelling is both viewed and taught in its proper context—that is, the context of purposeful writing—attention to the task will be distorted and the lessons learned in one setting (eg the spelling lesson) may not be fully used in another (free writing or message writing). Finally, although the processes of spelling and reading involve handling words in different ways, there are certainly some children who *are* able to learn about spelling from their experience of reading. The question of the interrelationship between spelling and the various other skill areas of the language arts is, therefore, an extremely important one—one to which I shall return in the section which follows.

SECTION TWO

RELATING SPELLING TO OTHER
LANGUAGE SKILLS

Spelling, Speaking and Listening

We have already seen from previous examples that the English writing system is not intended primarily as a phonetic system; it may be derived from the sound patterns of the language, but its goal is not to tell us how we should pronounce it (Albrow, 1974). There are indeed times, for example with a place name such as 'Milngavie' (pronounced 'Mill-guy'), that a teacher can bring relief to a child by saying, 'Yes, that's how we say the word, but this is how we write it'. For certain spelling anomalies this is the only good way to tackle learning. However, the system also has distinct advantages: the spelling of a given word will not change even though the word may be pronounced variously by different speakers in different parts of the country.

I would not want to suggest that the sound of the word or its spoken form is *not* important for the attention of the learner. The spelling of regular words can be aided considerably by attending closely to the sequence of the sounds as well as to the visual shape of the word, and certain mnemonics for use with irregular words can use sound to help to clue the spelling (eg, making a mental note to pronounce the 'c' when writing a word such as 'scintillating'). It is useful for learners to develop a habit of saying a word as they write it, whether aloud or subvocally: first, it ensures that they actually know the word they are intending to write (remember the example of 'speacist'/'species'); secondly, it forces attention to the constituent parts and to their correct order (eg 'ther-mo-meter'). When pupils are using this approach, however, clear and accurate articulation (though not a standard accent) will also be important.

Spelling and Handwriting

It is sometimes claimed that spelling words routinely is at heart a motor act of writing. We are all used to building motor memories: a highly familiar word will be typed as an integrated sequence of finger movements by an experienced typist; some people need to go

8

through the motions of dialling a frequently used telephone number before they can say the sequence of digits; how long does it take after transferring to an automatic car before we stop reaching for the clutch pedal?

I think it goes a bit far, however, to argue that spelling is *only* a motor skill. The victim of a car accident who loses both his arms may have become impaired as a pianist, but he will not have lost his skill as a musician; similarly, he will not have lost his ability to spell, though he may need to learn a completely new method of writing. Children who are presently in school may find in the future that they spend more time at a word processor than with a pen in their hands.

For the present, however, it is still the case that most material which children produce in schools is in handwritten form. This is true also of most of their output at home. It is through writing that these children will be learning to spell, whatever alternative secretarial skills they may acquire in later life. Developing a clear, fluent handwriting script is therefore crucial, not just in order to avoid additional mistakes (certain children can form the letter 'n' to look like 'h'; for some, the confusion between 'b' and 'd' is actually a confusion in letter formation), but also in helping children build clear memories of how particular words are produced in writing, and thus to assist them in making spelling automatic. This cannot occur where letters are poorly or irregularly formed.

It is for these reasons that most spelling manuals will stress that learning to spell should involve *writing* the words, not just saying the letters or sounds. Spelling machines or computer programmes which teach spelling may only require children to key the words on to the machine, but the children should also be encouraged at some point to write the same words on paper (Peters, 1985). I would go further and argue that, at some point in the process of studying new words, children should be asked to write them quickly and fluently. The closer the conditions of the learning context to the actual conditions of writing, the more effectively children will be able to use their learning in situations where they most require it.

Spelling and Reading

For some years now there have been people keen to argue that the English writing system should be simplified in order to make spelling easier. Certainly, children face a lot of difficulty when they try to tackle words such as 'oscillate' and 'quail'. As we have already seen, however, the spelling of a word tells us not just about its sound; it tells us a great deal more about its meaning, history, purpose and function. Not all of this information is important for the speller (although knowing the meaning and function can help in discriminating homonyms such as 'their' and 'there'), but it is extremely valuable for the reader. It would seem that any reform which would make spelling one step easier would make reading one step harder (Frith, 1985).

Beginning readers look closely at the details of the word but fluent readers rarely do. They use the clues from the context and the meanings of the words, together with their knowledge of what has gone before in the passage, to try to predict what is likely to come next. When they get to a word, all they need to do is check quickly whether it seems to fit with what they expected, and if so they can move on. The process of checking does not need to be too detailed, for what we tend to find is that when fluent readers do make mistakes, they produce errors which make sense in terms of the general gist of the passage and which look quite similar to the word which was intended. I recently listened to Andrew, an eleven year old who is good at reading for meaning. He read 'scarcely drawing a breath' for 'scarcely daring to breathe', a rendering which is hardly likely to affect his understanding of the passage, although three out of the four words had to be scored as errors.

The process of spelling is just the very opposite. As we saw in the opening section, it is not enough to produce a range of options, each of which sounds like the word in question. The task of spelling is to arrive at the only possible rendering for that one particular word. Nor are there many clues available to support the speller. Whereas the reader can ask, 'Does it build on what has gone before and does it make sense?', there is no such system of checking available when spelling. You are thrown back on your own skill as a speller and on the extent of your ability to recall, produce and recognise spelling which is accurate.

It is perhaps not surprising, then, that while most good readers are good spellers and most poor readers similarly poor spellers, there is a small group of children who are competent when they are reading but who struggle when they try to spell. Andrew is one such pupil. His preference in reading is to go straight from the print to the meaning. When I presented him with a series of nonsense words to spell, he tried to write them from visual memory without any attempt to say the words over to himself. Frith (1983) has suggested that pupils such as Andrew find it hard to go from print to sound, and they consequently have considerably greater difficulty with spelling than with reading. As if to emphasise that spelling and reading are discrete processes, there are even examples in the literature of children who can write words which they cannot read, and read words which they cannot write (see Bryant and Bradley, 1980).

Pupils who read predominantly for meaning and who pay little attention to word structure when they are looking at text are unlikely to gain much help with spelling from their experience of reading. There are other pupils, however, who *do* learn from their reading. In her study of young fluent readers, Margaret Clark found that many children who had become competent readers at an early age without having been taught specifically to read had also become good spellers (Clark, 1976). These are the children whom Margaret Peters would describe as having an ability to 'catch' spelling:

'For many (spelling) is 'caught' within the network of verbal skills which is the heritage of the linguistically favoured child. Such children want to communicate in writing and the urgency of their need provokes carefulness in spelling and handwriting. These children...look at words with interest, intent and intention to reproduce them correctly. They enjoy words, not only in context, but in structure....'

Peters and Cripps (1983), p 1.

Such children will be learning about word structure as they meet new words in reading. It is the children who do not share this interest, and who fail to absorb knowledge about spelling through their daily language encounters who require specific instruction, and for whom spelling must be 'taught'.

A final word about the relationship between reading and spelling. I have indicated that there are certain children who will be capable linguistically, but who, because of their preferred learning styles or because of certain inherent weaknesses, will have specific difficulties in the area of spelling. The proportion of these children is small. The great majority of poor spellers will also be poor readers, and they may, in addition, have rather limited verbal skills (for example, a restricted vocabulary). This must be considered when deciding on priorities for teaching. A child who regularly omits the initial consonant when attempting to spell may be in more urgent need of basic help with reading than with spelling. There is little point in teaching either reading or spelling if the words in question are words which the pupil does not yet know.

11

Spelling and Writing

'Even a casual analysis makes it clear that the number of things that must be dealt with simultaneously in writing is stupendous: handwriting, spelling, punctuation, word choice, syntax, textual connections, purpose, organisation, clarity, rhythm, euphony, the possible reactions of various readers, and so on. To pay conscious attention to all of these would overload the information processing capacity of the most towering intellects.'

Scardamalia, *in* Bereiter (1980), p 89.

Understanding how spelling relates to the act of composing (both for the learner and for the mature writer) is, perhaps, the most crucial aspect of the current section. Spelling is not an end in itself, it is a tool to aid the writer, yet ironically, more than any other aspect of writing, it is spelling which is frequently accused of interfering with the writer's craft. Teachers have even gone so far as to describe spelling and handwriting as 'the troublesome twins' of children's writing.

Where is it that the particular tensions lie? When can spelling be a help to the writer? Under what circumstances does attention to spelling begin to interfere with the process of composition? What strategies can both young and mature writers develop to help them in the double task of organising what they wish to say and communicating it successfully to a reader? Does the process of spelling in writing change as the writer becomes more skilled?

I have listed in the bibliography several valuable texts which outline how teachers can help children develop the ability to write. These stress that composing using written language is a highly intricate and complex process. Young children can learn the basics of individual writing skills, and they can be encouraged to develop an interest in using writing for purposes of genuine communication (for example, writing a message to someone who needs a piece of information and who has not received that information in any other way). There are certain types of writing, however, such as writing about emotion or writing to develop abstract, theoretical arguments, which can only be produced successfully by more mature language users. This is because writing is not an isolated skill but a complex, psychological activity, capable of being influenced by and, indeed, drawing upon various elements in the cognitive, linguistic, moral and emotional development of the writer. Mature writers need to be fluent in handling not just the *language* of writing but also certain ways of *thinking*.

12

I do not have space to develop this argument further, but it is important that as teachers we appreciate how complex written language production can be and how considerable are the achievements of young writers as they develop control of the medium. It is also important to appreciate that the writer who has a genuine message, who is struggling to give it expression and who is moved by a sense of urgency to share it, will be involved in a task which is qualitatively different from that of the pupil who is completing a routine, written exercise in class. This has important implications for the spelling: the level of the writer's involvement in the task, the presence (or lack) of a determination to get the message right for a reader, questions of vocabulary selection and the availability of opportunities to revise the writing will each have an influence on the type and amount of attention which may be given to spelling and on the accuracy of the results. Different tasks make different demands on the writer, and these can affect the success and handling of the spelling even for the most experienced writers.

Each of us will be conscious of making occasional spelling slips in writing, particularly if writing under pressure. These are the errors which are quickly spotted and easily corrected when we read back over the script. Recent studies of fluent writing have begun to suggest that these spelling slips may not be entirely random: there may be certain types of errors which occur quite regularly in the act of writing but which are unlikely to occur on a spelling test. A suggestion which has been put forward is that errors such as 'the/they' and 'country side/countryside' may be caused by a kind of whole word monitor in the writer's brain which reads over what is being produced and pushes the writer on to the next word as soon as the last one has been completed.* There could be some basis for this, for children make a lot of these kinds of mistakes, and they are far more likely to split a word if what is left is itself a whole word (eg 'time table' but not 'al ready'). If we knew more about the specific effects of the writing act on spelling and more about the types of execution errors which can commonly occur, then we could be more specific in encouraging pupils to check their writing for routine types of errors. It seems a fruitful line of research to be developed further.

Where writers are competent spellers, they will have a wide vocabulary available for easy use in writing, extending both their options and freedom as composers. Problems arise when children

* Sterling (1983).

13

lack spelling confidence. Not only can too much attention to spelling in the early stages of writing hamper their involvement in the more important task of selecting and organising their ideas, but concern for spelling may force them to stick with a rather 'safe' vocabulary, considerably restricting the range and colour of what will be produced. The quotation from Scardamalia stresses how difficult it is for young writers to develop an adequate level of competence in *each* of the areas required, while still attempting to tackle the larger question of learning how to compose. The solution seems to be to give separate attention to each of the various areas, but to start first with the most fundamental question—What is it that I am trying to say? Once the message has been established, the writer can be helped to revise it and polish it, and finally to sort out those features which can affect the presentation—including, of course, the spelling.

Separating the various processes will, therefore, help young learners to be able to develop the skills and confidence which they need in order to tackle a range of different types of writing. It is important, however, that we also give them opportunities to put these skills back together. Mature and flexible processing, which experienced writers are able to perform successfully and with some ease, is only possible once children have been given the chance to work with knowledge and understanding from a number of areas simultaneously.

It would appear from this discussion that the way in which a young speller handles spelling may be very different from the approach adopted by a more experienced writer. Even the mental processes involved in producing the word in writing may be qualitatively distinct.

Summary

No matter how beautiful the scene, or how accurate the colour reproduction, a photograph of a quaint country cottage will be marred if the verticals of the walls are not aligned with the frame of the picture. Approaching photography only with a concern to align the verticals, however, will produce few pictures of quality. Much the same could be said of spelling. If it becomes the principal concern when writing, then composition will suffer. But if it is neglected, then the final script will be marred for the reader, no matter how interesting or expressive the content. Let us be clear about this. I will stress frequently in the sections which follow that errors may need to be understood and tolerated as the learner

14

progresses towards fluency in handling written language. The goal, however, is to help children become competent and fluent spellers when producing original, meaningful writing.

There are parallels in the field of music. In order to master a particularly complicated passage in a piano composition, it may be necessary to stop playing the entire piece and to dissect the part which is giving most trouble. Right and left hands may be worked separately, runs repeated, speed deliberately altered to force attention to detail. Finally, however, the pianist puts aside these practice techniques and returns to the start of the piece, confident that when the same passage is reached it will be easier to play at the correct tempo, and that the player will be freed to pay more specific attention to aspects of musical interpretation and to the general contouring of the performance. Indeed, if a pianist is interpreting a piece with good feeling and a sensitive touch, then the listener will be able to tolerate the odd stumble without it distracting too greatly from the pleasure of the performance. There may be no such pleasure in a performance which, though technically brilliant, lacks evidence of musical sensitivity.

The parallels with spelling are obvious, save for one point. If a pianist could play a sequence of scales with precision and speed when practising but could not execute the same runs when these occurred in the middle of a performance, we should say that the pianist had not yet reached a true level of technical competence on the runs. Yet for too long we have been content to understand spelling not by looking at the skill as it is used in complex writing, but as we see it in the stylised practice arena—viz, the spelling lesson. The children, too, have accepted our perspective. To my astonishment, I hear first year secondary pupils tell me, 'I used to be good at spelling in primary school. We don't do spelling any more'.

Whatever may be illustrated in the sections which follow, the examples show that when they write children do, indeed, 'do spelling'. The accuracy of their attempts will depend not just on the level of spelling knowledge but on various demands of the writing task and on the writer's control over a large number of task features, including selection of vocabulary and opportunities for revision. I will offer various examples from classroom writing to illustrate these points. In the final section, I will develop implications of these analyses for questions of teacher practice both in primary and secondary schools.

SECTION THREE

UNDERSTANDING SPELLING IN THE SPELLING LESSON AND IN FLUENT WRITING

Learning from the Spelling Lesson

The spelling lesson may not be the best setting for making judgements about how well an individual uses skill in spelling when orchestrating a piece of writing. In the spelling lesson, specific attention is paid to the act of spelling, and words are selected for study by the teacher or the spelling manual, in some cases without regard to whether their meaning will be familiar to the learner. As the Bullock report warns,

> 'Children may be able to cope with all the words in a given list after concentrated study, but they may still fail with the same words when they come to use them in writing.'
>
> HMSO (1983), p 183.

This is not to say that there is not an important place for careful word study—there is—but success in the spelling lesson may not ensure success with the same words in writing. Interestingly, the converse also applies: problems in the spelling lesson may not signal gross failure in writing. An example illustrates. Kathleen and Jackie (both 11 years old and attending the same secondary school) produced the following attempts when asked to spell six words on a graded word spelling test:

KATHLEEN	JACKIE
reaier	reguare
otortagrath	otprape
grath	gragch
visical	vicice
canvafect	catastrath
crestent	cresent

The words, taken from the middle and end of the test, were 'require', 'autograph', 'gradually', 'physical', 'catastrophe' and 'crescent'. Looking at the girls' errors suggests that they may have some problems in auditory and visual sequencing (eg otprape/autograph, grath/gradually, vicice/physical), and, perhaps of greater concern,

16

only a limited understanding of the letter combinations which are permissible in English (eg 'gragch'). On the basis of such an analysis, we might suggest activities to encourage attention to auditory sequencing (eg tapping out syllables, rhyming exercises), visual sequencing (eg training attention to the visual image of a word), and common letter patterns (eg generating possible spellings for nonsense words). First, however, we need to consider the spelling performance of the same two girls in their general class writing, and here there are some surprises: in a single week both girls made fewer than 6% of spelling errors in all the writing which they produced across the different subjects. One of the tasks was a piece of narrative writing entitled 'From Fear to Safety.' On this task, Kathleen wrote 130 words and Jackie 180, and the only errors which they made were as follows:

KATHLEEN	JACKIE
dont/don't	mum/Mum's
throuth/through	knive/knife
stil/still	reliefed/relieved
to/told	

It would appear that when the girls had freedom to select the vocabulary to be used on a real writing task, they made spelling errors which were less severe than in a situation where they could not exercise such a choice, and their errors could still be recognised as the intended word. The example seems to suggest that it is hard to draw firm conclusions based on children's spelling errors unless you take into account why the writing was produced, who provided the vocabulary, the complexity and range of the vocabulary, and how familiar and relevant it was to the writer. It also suggests that, given a degree of freedom over their material, these particular girls could cope perfectly adequately with the twin demands of spelling and writing in their ordinary classwork. (Note, however, that this situation would not arise with children still to develop a basic competence in spelling; both these girls could spell many of the earlier words on the test correctly).

Generalising from the Spelling Lesson

It is, of course, unusual to think of children being more successful spellers in their ordinary classwork than in the spelling lesson. We are more familiar with the situation where the opposite occurs, where the word is studied and learned but subsequently misspelled when it comes up again in writing. There can be many reasons for

17

this. First, not all learning sticks, so the word may be forgotten even when tested in a subsequent spelling lesson. More fundamentally, the act of producing spelling when writing for meaning is in many respects different from producing spelling in a spelling lesson, since there are competing demands within the writing task to consider content, to plan ahead, to attend to form, expression and style (and so forth). Successful spelling in a writing context, therefore, must not only be accurate but relatively *automatic*, requiring a minimum of sustained effort and attention on the part of the writer.

Because the writing task is so much more complex, it has been harder for researchers to look at what happens to the spelling of particular words after children have studied them in the spelling lesson. The words may never be used again. They may be used correctly in classwork only because they are written on the blackboard or displayed on the wall as spelling aids. On some occasions a child may use a given word correctly, at other times incorrectly. A child may even improve in ability to spell other (new) words by drawing analogies based on knowledge of the particular words that have been studied. Not surprisingly, quantifying these influences is difficult, and so there is little guidance available to teachers to help them to know what to expect in terms of spelling from a particular child in a particular writing situation.

There is a clear challenge for researchers to find ways of examining the systematic influences on spelling in real writing tasks. One such approach is the use of case study, valuable since detailed information can be collected under controlled circumstances from a number of settings (the spelling lesson, the writing situation etc.) and examined closely for evidence of systematic changes over time. A case study can suggest certain trends and connections, it cannot prove them; similarly, though trends may be shown to hold true for a particular individual, these may not be true for all other writers. The principal value of the case study approach, applied to an area as intricate as spelling, is that it allows for close examination of interrelating aspects of the task which might otherwise remain confusing and elusive. Understanding something of the complexity of the task of spelling can be an important step for teachers in appreciating the achievements and frustrations of children as they write.

Case Study: The Spelling Lesson and Speed Writing

This case study, which throws light on some of the influences on spelling accuracy in children's ordinary writing, was conducted to examine the changes in spelling which could occur in a boy's personal story writing*. The investigation took place over a period of months, at a time when the particular pupil was known to be making good progress in specific study of spelling.

David was 12 years old, good at practical subjects, acknowledged by his teachers to have a sound grasp of concepts and ideas in subjects such as History and Geography, but dogged throughout his schooling by difficulties with reading and spelling. An example of his response on an S1 Geography examination is given in Figure 1.

Despite longstanding difficulties in handling textual language, David still took a keen interest in words, and under the guidance of one particular teacher had developed a taste for writing poetry. His outstanding area of achievement was Art, and throughout the period of the study he consistently led his year group in assessed work in this subject.

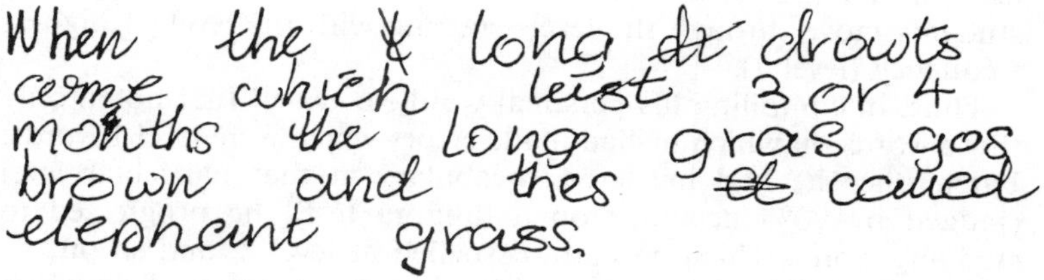

Figure 1—An Example of David's Writing in School, taken from a first year geography examination script.

It had come to David's notice that he would not get into Art school without a pass in English, and so it was at his own request that a home tuition programme was started. Since both he and the school were satisfied that he was finally making progress in reading, the programme was aimed specifically at providing him with the knowledge, skills and tools to improve his spelling when engaged in fluent writing.

I conducted the sessions at David's home, twice a week, and the contact extended over seven months. There were two distinct parts to the programme which I offered: fifteen minutes of formal spelling tuition (the spelling lesson) and ten minutes of continuous writing (known as speed writing).

In the spelling lessons, five words a session were studied from

* A full report of the study, together with statistical details, is provided in Chapter 9 of Barr (1983) and elsewhere (Barr, in press). Only the information that is necessary for understanding and interpreting the findings will be outlined here.

David's personal wordlist, built up from words which he had already tried to write in school, but failed to use correctly. This approach ensures a general link between the vocabulary studied in the spelling lessons and the pupil's wider writing needs. There was an added refinement, since the wordlist was also constructed so as to include at first only those words of highest frequency: David would begin by studying vocabulary that was common (even if difficult to spell), which he would need to use regularly and which would offer, following learning, repeated opportunities for practice and revision. On this approach, only once he had mastered those words would he go on to study a more specialised vocabulary.

There are a number of published wordlists which group words by frequency of usage and which can assist in such a task. In this study, I chose to use the *Alphabetical Spelling Lists* published by Wheaton (1977), because these lists arrange the 2,700 words most frequently used in children's writing into seven levels of frequency, and students move through the levels starting with the level of highest frequency (level 1).

Thus, in compiling his personal wordlist, David first noted only those words on which he had made errors which were level 1 words. Later, once he had mastered vocabulary at that particular level (judged by 90% accuracy on a random test), he progressed to studying words which he had misspelled at level 2, and so on.

During the fifteen minute spelling lesson a number of activities took place:

(i) I tested David on the five words that had been studied in the previous session. He wrote his answers from dictation, and kept a record of the scores. If he was still unsure of the spelling of a particular word, it would be studied again subsequently.

(ii) Five new words were selected from the personal wordlist to be learned that session. David was trained to use the procedure *look/say/cover/write/check*, and he was encouraged to study each new word carefully, where appropriate breaking the word into component parts, identifying areas of difficulty, and using finger tracing (with and without eyes shut). Only when he was confident that he had learned the word did he write it in the first column of a 4-column sheet of paper. After carefully checking that he was correct, he repeated this three more times, folding the paper so as to be sure to be writing from memory on each occasion.

20

Such an approach is generally eclectic, involving various senses and including opportunities for overlearning. Where it was appropriate to study a particular word not as an isolated case but as an instance of a particular word pattern (eg 'could', 'would', 'should'), we would look together at the group of words bearing the pattern, but the emphasis both in studying and in subsequent testing was still on the original study word.

(iii) Once the words had been learned, David wrote them carefully from dictation in his learned list (a record of words studied). He then attempted to construct a coherent sentence to include all five words. While such an activity is by no means obligatory in a spelling programme nor desirable for certain children, it appealed to David's particular interest in playing with words, and he set himself the challenge of constructing a meaningful sentence with the minimum of additional words.

(iv) Finally, I gave David a two-minute speed test, presenting the five words studied that session in any order, to be written as fast as he could manage. He kept a graph that recorded the total written correctly in the two minutes, and the challenge lay in attempting to increase the score from session to session. The main value of such an exercise is that it provides practice in writing these newly learned words quickly, automatically and with accuracy.

There will be teachers who will question elements of this approach, who may favour a different rationale for selecting vocabulary or a greater emphasis on exercises and/or rules. The approach adopted was in many respects tailored to David's particular situation: he had already experienced several years of spelling failure despite regular tuition, and I was concerned to find an approach that would give him greatest control over his own learning, together with sound strategies for word study and a rationale for knowing where to start and how to proceed. As the Bullock report urges:

'With regard to spelling. . .we believe the most important step the teacher can take is to improve the pupil's confidence in his own capacity.'

HMSO (1975), p 167.

Measures which were taken over the period of the study suggest that the approach did indeed have something to offer David. When first tested on words randomly selected from the levels of the *Alphabetical Spelling Lists*, he scored 72% at level 1. Accordingly, he began his word study at this level, studying 28 words over six sessions. When next tested on a different selection of level 1 words (taken from the entire list, not just from those words studied) he achieved a score of 96% and so progressed to words at level 2. He studied 126 words at this level over 30 sessions, achieving scores on successive level 2 tests of 48%, 76%, 80% and 88%, at which point he progressed to words at level 3. He scored between 76% and 80% on three tests at level 3, studied 79 words at this level and was still on level 3 when the programme ended.

Separate evidence from the speed tests showed that while in the early sessions David wrote around 10 words correctly in the two minute period, by the end of the programme he was averaging 14 words per session, indicating an increase in either speed of production, spelling accuracy, or both.

A more independent measure was the Daniels and Diack graded word test with Schonell supplement (Peters, 1970), which I administered at the start and finish of the programme. David was 12 years 5 months when first tested, and he wrote 25 of the words correctly, achieving a spelling age of 7.8 years. When retested at 13 years he scored 38 words, which gives a spelling age of 11.0 years, and indicates an improvement of 3.2 years in spelling age over the seven consecutive months of the programme.

The decision to stop the formal programme was made jointly by David and myself. We had not been seeing evidence of progress on the home tuition programme alone. David had also been improving in his performance in a number of subjects in school, and by the middle of his second year had so outstripped his fellow pupils in the Remedial English class that he was promoted back into the mainstream. Since this meant that he was now starting to learn French in a class where the subject had already been studied for four terms, we agreed that this was a good point at which to draw the formal spelling tuition sessions to a close.

The spelling lesson was, however, only one element in the programme. The other component was speed writing. Pupils who have persistent spelling difficulties frequently write very little when given the opportunity, either because they find writing hard (spelling difficulties *can* make the task of writing harder) or because they have learned over the years that if you want to avoid the teacher's pen, you write little and you keep it simple. Thus, many of these pupils learn to take as few risks and experiment as little in writing as possible.

22

David was no exception. Despite obvious enthusiasm in exploring and discussing ideas, when he put pen to paper he kept his statements brief, vocabulary simple, and the handwriting at times 'ambiguous' (possibly as a disguise for his uncertainty over spelling). What he needed was practice in fluency, and this was what the speed writing sessions were designed to encourage.

These are the instructions which I gave to David concerning speed writing:

    (i)   Select a topic to write about.
    (ii) Set the kitchen timer for 10 minutes.
    (iii) Write as much as you can on the topic, starting immediately.
    (iv) Stop as soon as the timer goes off.
    (v) Count the number of words you have written, and enter the number on the chart which you are keeping.

I stressed that the main aim of this exercise was to write as much as possible on the chosen topic, without paying too much attention to accuracy of spelling, grammar and letter formation. I did not mark the stories, nor did I draw attention to the spelling, and in this respect the speed writing sessions were run independently of the spelling lessons. From time to time we read the stories together and discussed the ideas which they generated.

This again is not an activity which I would recommend for all pupils. As an exercise it is meaningful and samples of the writing comparable only if the pupil is genuinely interested in the writing, and if that interest can be sustained over the sessions. For David, it was an activity which had an immediate (and lasting) appeal, and this justified its inclusion in the present study. Over the seven month period, David produced a total of 40 scripts. Other children I have worked with have been less enthusiastic and less willing to persevere over a much smaller number of sessions.

Speed writing had certain benefits for David. It also had certain benefits for myself as researcher, since with a total of 40 stories, produced under similar conditions, comparisons could be made and vocabulary and spelling analysed to look for trends and developments in David's writing over the period of the study. As I have pointed out, the influence of the spelling lesson may be hard to detect in isolated pieces of classwork. Over 40 scripts, however, systematic changes may become apparent, even though the step size in the change from script to script is small.

Forty speed writing scripts were available to be analysed, produced over a period when David was systematically working

23

through a programme of spelling tuition. I knew that when he was formally tested he showed evidence of improvement in spelling over this period. I also knew which words he had been studying in the spelling lessons. Would there be a comparable improvement in spelling in the speed writing scripts? Would it be specific to certain types of vocabulary? Were there other systematic changes in the writing which would emerge over the period?

Here, an added benefit of using the *Alphabetical Spelling Lists* emerges. By putting all 2,700 words from the lists on to the computer together with an indication of each word's frequency level (1-7), and by creating a new category level (level 8) for any word not already on the lists, it becomes possible to write a programme which can analyse any given text in terms of the frequency of the vocabulary which is used. Add to that an indication of correct and incorrect spelling, and you have a powerful and flexible computer programme which can tell you not only how complex is the writer's choice of vocabulary, but how successful is his handling of spelling on different types of words. Fuller details of the programme are given in Barr (1983) and Lambourne and Barr (1984).

I typed each of the forty stories on to the computer and identified any spelling errors. The computer analysis then made it possible to look story by story at the following aspects of the writing:

(i) The number of words written during the ten minutes available for speed writing.
(ii) The number of words written at each of the different frequency levels (1-8).
(iii) The number of words that were misspelled.
(iv) The distribution of misspellings across the various frequency levels of vocabulary.

Stories produced towards the beginning of the programme could then be compared with stories written towards the end to ask the following questions:

(i) Is there a change across the stories in the total number of words written?
(ii) Is there a change across the stories in the number and proportion of words written at the different levels of vocabulary frequency?
(iii) Is there a change across the stories in the number and proportion of spelling errors at the different levels of vocabulary frequency?

24

More specific questions could be asked about how David handled selected words in speed writing (eg vocabulary known to have been studied in the spelling lessons) and about the general relevance of adopting an approach to word study which is based on the principle of word frequency.

The results are interesting. Over the period of the programme, David increased steadily the number of words which he wrote in the ten minute session—that is, in the later stories he was writing more and he was writing at a faster rate. In addition, he began to use a much more varied and complex vocabulary: in early stories, he used few words at levels 4-7, but the amount and proportion of these low-frequency words increased over the period of the study. Since he was not only writing faster but was using a richer, more varied and more complex vocabulary (with, remember, no opportunities to correct his work after the ten minute session was finished), we might understand if these changes resulted in a slight increase in the proportion of spelling errors in the later stories. This was not however the case. Overall there was shown to be a slight decrease in the proportion of errors (22% in the first ten stories, 17% in the last ten), but the interesting insights came from a closer examination of what was happening to the spelling of words at the different levels of vocabulary frequency.

Level 1 words, the most common words, accounted for the majority of what was written, and David made the smallest proportion of errors on these particular words. On level 2, however, he started by writing more words incorrectly than correctly, and this continued until story 17 when the tendency was reversed (despite the fact that by then he was using many more words at level 2 than in his earlier stories). A similar picture emerges for level 3: initially there were very few of these words; for a period more words were spelled incorrectly than correctly; then from story 21 onwards more level 3 words were used and a greater proportion was spelled correctly. The same pattern emerges for level 4 (although the total number of words used at this level was small), with signs of improvement occurring around story 29. More words were consistently spelled incorrectly than correctly at the other levels of the *Alphabetical Spelling Lists* (levels 5-7).

These results suggest that there *is* a place for considering vocabulary frequency, if the hope is to aid spelling efficiency on real writing tasks. The frequency levels of the *Alphabetical Spelling Lists* were borne out in David's own writing: he wrote most words at level 1, fewer at level 2, fewer still at level 3. Conversely, the highest proportion of errors was made on the least common vocabulary (words at level 7). Evidence from changes which occurred in the writing is also relevant: David's own spelling showed the first signs of improvement on words at level 2, then came changes at level 3, lastly at level 4. Of course, this is the same as the sequence of study followed in the spelling lessons, but it appears that what we are looking at is not something that was merely controlled by the spelling lessons themselves, since the stories were employing a much more varied vocabulary, even within frequency levels. In addition, the timescale of the improvement in speed writing did not coincide exactly with the phases of the spelling lessons: improvement in speed writing at level 2 came only after words at level 2 had been studied for some time and continued after those words were no longer being studied; the improvement at level 3 occurred before the move to level 3 in the spelling lessons; the spelling lessons never dealt with words at level 4. Finally, it is useful to look at how David handled in speed writing those words which had already been studied in the spelling lessons: of the 28 words studied at level 1, 43% appeared in the last ten speed writing stories; of the 126 from level 2, only 15%; and of the 79 from level 3, only 8%. Of these, around two thirds of the words at level 1, a little under half the words at level 2, and only a third of the words at level 3 were spelled correctly when used subsequently in speed writing.

It's a complex picture, but a clear one. The high frequency words as defined by the *Alphabetical Spelling Lists* emerged as those which David used most in his free writing, which he learned with greatest efficiency, and whose spelling, once learned, he remembered best. These are also, by definition, the words on which he would get most opportunities for practice and for feedback in his general classwork. Once improvement was established on these very common words, signs of a similar improvement emerged for the less common vocabulary. There were also signs that David's spelling improved on a wider vocabulary than had been studied in the spelling lessons.

The evidence of improvement in spelling in this study is encouraging. Not only was David becoming more accurate in his spelling, but he was writing more, writing faster, and using a richer vocabulary. Three sample scripts (taken from the beginning, middle and end of the study) are reproduced in Figure 2, and these give a flavour of some of the changes that occurred. Remember that speed writing was produced under strict time pressure, without

26

opportunities to revise or edit, and so understandably contains a higher proportion of errors (including errors of execution) than would be expected in a polished piece of work.

There are clear lessons for teachers from a case study such as this, and even some warnings. In absolute numbers, there were more spelling errors in the later stories because more was being written. There were also more bizarre errors, since errors were more likely to be made on unusual vocabulary (eg 'palace', 'furious', 'magician',

(a) One day I want home and I saw an annimapricols when I got close to it its back lege was reed so I got in the annimapricolses house and tuck out a leef from the aid first box but when I game out of the house he was hopping and skipping so I put it back and went home ther I sow my dad wreading a paper and on the front of it was a picher of an annimapricols with a red leg, I pinned it up.

(NOTE: an annimapricols is a term invented by David to describe an imaginary animal)

(b) Magic is a very spectionet thing as the quicker it's don the beter it is so you hafed to work fast enough to be good but not so fast that the people dont see what you are doing so you yousley speek to the ordense and tell them what you are doing in the akt as the people who are washing are not magitions so they do not no the akt thats you must tork to the people so if you want to do magic dont forget to speak as you go along with the akt and you also need a top hat and a big box to

(c) Long, Long, Long ago be for the word began there lived a king. Also there was an evil wizard meny of the people and bed killed by him the wizard sent a mesige to the king saing = I have invented a thing called wind this wind will distroy the how of your castle if you dont give me harf the kindom and the palis. the king was furios and sent all the brave knight and barons of the land to fight the eivl wizard but the night could fight the wind as they could not se it. all the king wise mand and magistin cam and trid to think of a way to get rid of the wind. Then a nothe leter came from the wizard saying the whind is in a box and if I let them all out they

Figure 2—Three Speed Writing Stories by David, written (a) at the beginning, (b) in the middle and (c) at the end of the study.

'knight' in the third story in Figure 2). If you were to look only at the errors without taking into account either how much was written or the changes in the language that was used (including, arguably, changes in the quality of what was produced), then you would underestimate the very real achievement of the writer and might even run the risk of discouraging his efforts. Similarly, if you were watching for words which had been studied in the spelling lessons and were hoping for accurate recall, this study suggests you would be disappointed: even words at level 1 contained several errors in the speed writing stories, though in the test situation they were almost invariably written correctly; the majority of level 3 words which had been carefully studied in the spelling lesson were still misspelled when used subsequently in speed writing. Yet the study does not suggest that David was not improving as a speller over the period of the programme. On the contrary, in both the spelling lessons and the speed writing sessions he showed a consistent move towards greater confidence in handling vocabulary. It takes, however, the careful analysis of a collection of stories which have been produced under similar writing conditions to show the systematic changes which were taking place—changes which can give the teacher confidence to accept the pupil's attempts as an improving speller and developing writer.

There is an interesting trend in David's use of vocabulary which is useful for us to note, although on a single case we can only be tentative in the conclusions which we draw. I have pointed out that there was a two-fold improvement on some of the less common vocabulary, with more words being used latterly and more correctly. At each level, however, there were two distinct stages as the improvement occurred: first, there was a period when substantially more words were being used but where there was an increase in the proportion of spelling errors; only once the increase in word use was established did the improvement then follow in spelling accuracy. On a task as complex as writing, are there perhaps some children for whom this first stage of improvement in one aspect of the task associated with a temporary deterioration in other aspects is a *necessary* stage before improvement can be demonstrated across a range of performance features?

Perhaps there is a more fundamental question here. It could be that the speed writing programme was not simply 'tapping' David's improving spelling knowledge, but in a real sense contributing to it, by providing frequent and regular opportunities to use vocabulary in writing, under time pressure and in conditions where attention to spelling was not the primary consideration. Such an exercise may help the process of making spelling knowledge automatic. Children may not learn to use certain words correctly or fluently in writing until they are provided with opportunities to try out the use of these words on genuine writing tasks.

Summary: Influences on Spelling in Writing

In this section I have touched on a number of the difficulties which can face teachers as they try to respond to children's spelling in their general writing. Although children may be improving in their spelling knowledge, and although this improvement may be reflected over a period of time in their day-to-day writing, the changes may not be immediately obvious: errors will still be made (even on words which the children have studied specifically) and new errors can creep in as the vocabulary demands of the task increase. The case study of David shows how important it is to take into account the circumstances of the writing (eg rate of production, opportunities for revision and review) and the type of vocabulary used (common, familiar words or more adventurous words and expressions) before passing judgement on the spelling performance in the writing. Responding to and encouraging development of a whole number of aspects of writing is a highly delicate task.

There is some indication in the evidence from the case study that children may need permission to explore, experiment and make errors in their writing before they can learn to use certain words freely, with accuracy and with confidence. Some implications of this for the teachers (who structure the pupils' writing experiences) and for the pupils (who not only produce the writing but can subject it to revision and review) will be considered more fully in the final section.

SECTION FOUR

UNDERSTANDING SPELLING IN DIFFERENT KINDS OF WRITING

Introduction

Three boys, top infants in an English primary school, produced the following pieces of writing:

PHILIP (7y 6m)

(1) Have you seen our postman? He is coming with letters and a small preasnt fore me. I shall keep the box till Thursday. That is the day of my birthday.

(2) 1. The sweet was round.
2. It smells like orange.
3. We un-rapped it by our ears.
4. It did tased nice.
5. My tased buds did tingle.
6. Inside the hard sweet it was soft.
7. I don't no if it was frait inside.

CHRISTOPHER (7y 1m)

(1) Havo you see a men. he is cumiing and a illtt I shall keep the Box til

(2) it is clue and it is browen it tasst lilok tof

PAUL (7y 5m)

(1) Have you seen our postman? He is coming with letters and a small prestent for me. I shell ceap The box untill Thursday. That is the day of my Birthday.

(2) Eckspermenting. Jenefer said it loocked like a dogs face pernsle I thort it Loocked like the top of a moter bike controll panull The paper soundid Like The Sea on the out side it was ruff on the in side of the paper was stike the sweet was made By needlers LtD. smell Like Lime it was sticke and it tasted like Lime and as hard as rock you have to suck er fingers it wood get hot if you helled it for a long tim it allso lik look a cake and an old fasand car wheel and a pot it

30

> looked Lime flaverd Lime flaverd things vooselle come in
> green culler it allso loocked Like an aming thing in Uboats
> it cood be a frisdre.

Three boys, writing on two tasks, producing pieces of writing that
differ in a number of important respects.

The first task was a piece of dictation. Both Philip and Paul
coped well on this task, and there is little to distinguish their
attempts. In both cases, although there are some spelling errors, the
reader can still follow the meaning of the text. For Christopher,
however, the demands of the task were more than he could handle
successfully. Several words are missed out, the sense is lost and
attempts to spell certain words (eg illtt/letter) are hard to decode.
It's not just the new reader who would find this writing difficult:
after any lapse of time, Christopher himself would be unlikely to be
able to read it and get much sense from it.

The second task was a piece of writing describing what the
children had seen, felt and tasted as they unwrapped and ate a
sweet. Here each boy could select his own vocabulary, and decide
how much he would write and what detail to include. Again,
Christopher's statement is the shortest, but it is a more successful
and a more fluent piece of writing than he managed on the
dictation. A reader might have trouble coping with his attempted
spellings, but Christopher himself would probably be able to read
his writing back ('It is curly and it is brown. It tastes like toffee.')

Philip, by contrast, was able to be more adventurous in his
response on this task. He organised his writing well, listed points,
cited different types of evidence and established a nice sense of the
narrator as the experiencer ('Inside the hard sweet it was soft. I
don't know if it was fruit inside'.)

Philip and Paul may have been comparable in their performance
on the dictation task, but it is on this second task (the task offering
greater scope and freedom to the writer) that Paul was able to
demonstrate just how comfortably he could use written language to
convey vivid imagination and insight. Even his opening statements
('Experimenting. Jennifer said it looked like a dog's face. Personally
I thought it looked like the top of a motor bike control panel. . . .')
reveal a familiarity with the style and conventions of written
language which few seven-year-olds succeed in mastering. Even
fewer possess the detailed knowledge of vocabulary and grammar
which can allow them to use the written medium to develop and
express their ideas so freely.

31

These, then, are examples of two writing tasks which place different demands on different writers and which offer differing chances for success. Spelling is not the only feature to be considered, but even a brief glance at the boys' attempts shows that the different tasks (and how the boys chose to interpret these tasks) placed their own constraints on the accuracy of the spelling. Christopher could cope better when he was allowed to choose his words, and when he kept the writing simple. By contrast, Paul could spell adequately on a dictation passage, but made many more errors on the free writing task because he elected to write a lot and to use a rich and varied vocabulary.

In this section we will explore some of the influences, pressures and constraints that are associated with different types of writing, and look at how these can affect spelling accuracy in the classwork of different children.

Making Comparisons across Different Types of Writing

A study which I conducted in nine schools in England and New Zealand looked specifically at how groups of 'better' and 'poorer' spellers (all eleven year olds, and all capable of handling different types of writing successfully) performed on a number of *different* writing tasks. The study goes into greater detail than we need to consider here, although those who are interested can find fuller accounts in Barr (1983) and Barr and Lambourne (1984).

Three main findings emerged concerning influences on spelling accuracy in the writing. First, the distinction in the study between good and poor spellers (made initially on the basis of a proof-reading spelling test) was borne out in the children's performance on *each* of the writing tasks: whether the task offered help or no help with the spelling, and whether the vocabulary required was straightforward or complex, the group of good spellers achieved more accurate spelling in every instance than the group of poor spellers. The differences between good and poor spellers was not consistent, however. Where pupils could use vocabulary that was highly familiar to them or where a particular task offered some help with the spelling (eg a question-answer sheet to accompany an information booklet), poorer spellers could draw on this advantage to improve their performance quite considerably. On these occasions their spelling was almost as good as that of the better spellers. Where these poor spellers were most exposed was on tasks where there was no such assistance available, where the requirement to use specific words was high and where the vocabulary itself was specialised. The implication seems clear: place too many demands on writers who already have difficulties in a certain area (eg spelling) and their performance may break down on a number of fronts; offer resources to support the area where the difficulty is the greatest, and these same pupils may produce pieces of writing that are both adequate and competent.

A second finding was that a very powerful influence on the spelling accuracy of *all* the children came from the demands of the task itself. Good spellers may achieve 91% accuracy on task A and poor spellers 87%, but on task B the good spellers may only manage 86%, and the poorer group a meagre 71%. Therefore, although it may be possible for teachers to find certain trends in the spelling performance of different groups of children on real writing tasks, we need to be cautious when seeking to draw conclusions that are based solely on these trends. Comparisons between the spelling abilities of different pupils will be fairest when they are based on writing which has been produced under similar conditions. Judgements about the spelling competence of a particular individual will need to take into account the difficulty level of the task(s), and how successfully the child can cope with a variety of demands in different types of writing.

The third finding is of particular interest to our consideration of influences on spelling in writing. Even though all the pieces of writing in this study drew on a common core vocabulary (they were part of a unit of work on Hong Kong), a major influence on the accuracy of the children's spelling was whether or not they could select for themselves the words which they needed to use. If the task had already prescribed the vocabulary for writing (eg a passage of dictation or a written description of a tape-slide sequence) the children made a greater number of errors; if they could choose their own words (eg a piece of story writing based only loosely on the topic) the spelling proved to be more efficient. At one level what the children were doing was obvious: where they could, they tended to select an easier, more familiar group of words to write. Yet even taking that into account, when they *did* use unusual vocabulary, it was better spelled on the tasks where they had the greatest amount of choice. This seems to suggest that where they are given the freedom, children will select vocabulary with which they are reasonably comfortable and which they feel confident they can use successfully. There may, in addition, be benefits for spelling where children can increase their control over *other* features of the writing.

Appreciating the Demands of Different Writing Tasks

We can see from the preceding examples that different kinds of task place different demands on the writer—not just in terms of spelling, but in terms of a number of features of composition. Successful spellers and competent writers will be able to handle these differences with ease. Younger learners and older, struggling writers may have relatively greater difficulty.

Let us look at some common, school-based writing tasks to try to appreciate a few of the constraints which these highly familiar activities can place on the young or struggling learner.

Dictation

Teachers in the primary and secondary sectors are often aware that free writing can be difficult for many children, particularly if the purpose of the writing is to provide a record from which ideas can later be revised. In an attempt to help the pupils, the teacher may prefer to dictate a set of notes. From the point of view of spelling, however, this is one task which places heavy constraints on the writer: the vocabulary has been selected not by the writer but by someone else, and the writer has no option but to use it. The moral seems clear. If the teacher is not testing spelling (a legitimate role for dictation), and if the aim is to produce writing which the pupil can consult later as a basis for learning (*and* if there are good reasons why the teacher has not already provided this material for the pupils in some readily available form), then any vocabulary in the dictated passage which may be hard, unfamiliar or specialised should be on view or on hand for easy pupil reference. Even secondary pupils may still need opportunities and encouragement after the passage has been dictated to check over their work and to consult about words on which they are still unsure.

Copying

In dictation the words are presented aurally, not visually. This is only one feature of the task. Another is that the writing is conducted under a degree of time pressure, particularly where a whole class is involved in the activity. This time pressure can be just as much of a problem where the task involves copying, especially since poor spellers or writers who lack confidence may be attempting to copy not phrase by phrase or even word by word but letter by letter. In one secondary school where I was surveying written work during a sample week, a classical studies teacher had required all pupils in three first year classes to copy a passage 110 words long from a worksheet. Despite the fact that all the words required for the writing were there on the worksheet, the pace of the activity had clearly been too much for one pupil, whose attempt to write the first four sentences reads as follows:

> Early in 44 BC 60 conspirator led. By An Ex tribune called Gaius and Marcus Junius Brutus Another Goverment offical PlaNNED to murderd himself King. Even to day no ONE knows if He did. To make Him self king. They waited UNtil until the Ides of march.

Along with other problems, this girl had difficulty scanning the passage to be copied, even although it was placed in front of her on the desk. Other pupils may be able to cope adequately when the passage is directly before them, but will have greater difficulty when the position is changed, for example when the model is written on a blackboard, poster or overhead projector. Each of these factors has implications for spelling accuracy, if only because the added difficulties may force a greater number of execution errors. In the copying task, as in dictation, vocabulary is preselected for the writer and may not always be familiar.

Short Answer Tasks and the Problems of Specialised Vocabulary

It may seem that these are small points to be emphasising, but a disturbing feature of children's school-based writing is just how much of the daily diet seems to consist of dictation, copying and short answers to highly structured questions. The Inspectors visiting a sample of Scottish primary schools reported in 1980 that in 33% of classes for 8 year olds, and 40% of classes for 11 year olds, continuous writing of any form appeared to take place only once every two or three weeks (HMSO, 1980). After similar investigations in secondary schools two years later, both Ernest Spencer and Margaret Clark and her colleagues claimed that over half of all the pupil writing which took place in class was either copied or dictated, and the bulk of the remainder took the form of short answers to questions on worksheets (Spencer, 1983; Clark, Barr and McKee, 1982).

Even with worksheets there can be pitfalls for the speller. True, there is help available to guide spelling on many of the words (the help is often in the question itself), but structured questions can also limit the options which are open to pupils when they are answering. An example will help. On a worksheet presented to a first year secondary science class there was the following question, with one line provided for the answer:

All living things must reproduce themselves. Why?

A successful answer to this question has to indicate in an appropriate fashion that reproduction is a means of ensuring that the species will not become extinct. The worksheet excuses pupils from having to write their answer as a complete sentence, and they do not have to go into any great detail. However, it is that very detail which can often support the less confident writers, since they may use expansion, repetition and redundancy in their descriptions to show that they understand the concepts involved, even although they may not be wholly familiar with the vocabulary which most aptly summarises those concepts. Similarly, a whole sentence response to a set question can give the writer a certain amount of support and success in structuring a fluent written statement (in this instance the answer might start, 'The reason why all living things must reproduce themselves is..'). What pupils are left with in the present example is a pass/fail situation where supports for the writer have been systematically stripped away, and where the only information which the pupils are to give is the very information on which there are no clues in the question. The pupils may know the answer, but to be successful they must be able to communicate that knowledge briefly, concisely and in writing.

A number of the children in this class did know the answer but were unsure how to spell the word 'species'. One girl covered herself successfully in the wording of her reply:

To prevent there speacist (type of living thing) from be coming extinct.

This girl knew that, despite the problems of the task, the teacher was not really interested in testing her spelling knowledge at this point. Had the word 'species' come up in a spelling test, she would have been unlikely to have answered in this manner.

Another girl experienced greater difficulty, despite still being aware of the information. In her failing attempts to find an alternative expression for 'species', her response collapses into incoherence:

They prevent theirselfs to prevent there from Ecommetaterd extent.

The worksheet format is often defended as offering a useful

method for pupils to rehearse their knowledge and for teachers to check what has been mastered. It will do this. But it will also place subtle demands which may make it harder for pupils to demonstrate knowledge which they have actually acquired. If what they really need is practice in making use of that knowledge (fitting it in with other ideas, putting it into their own words) then a more flexible task may be required.

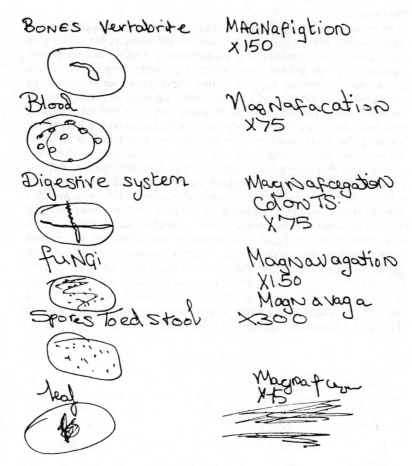

Figure 3—Various Attempts at Spelling the Term 'Magnification', taken from the science worksheet of an eleven year old boy.

As we have seen in this example, pupils may also need specific help in learning how to handle the specialist vocabulary of a particular topic or subject, especially how to handle it in writing. Such terms frequently have no well-known alternative forms of expression, and they can pose recurring problems for a writer, even when that writer is as resourceful and persevering as is indicated in Figure 3.

Summary

In this section I have been looking at some of the pressures on writers from the constraints inherent in different types of writing task. Dictation, copying, and short answer writing are all highly familiar tasks for school-age children. Of course, they can be useful for achieving certain purposes, but these purposes may not be sufficient to justify the disproportionate amount of time which is currently spent on such writing by many pupils in our schools. Not only may the tasks themselves present difficulties which may make learning the facts and concepts harder, but too much practice at these types of writing may be depriving pupils of the very experiences that they need in order to improve their skills as writers. Children need freedom to explore, experiment and make errors in order to learn—in writing as in any other area. There is a paradox here: in trying to help by simplifying the task for those who can find writing difficult, we are removing the vital element of the children's own control over the task. Furthermore, we reduce in the process their opportunities for developing success through free and frequent use of writing for genuine and practical purposes. The irony is that the very children who can make best use of dictation, copying and short answer writing for the purposes for which we claim to use them in the classroom are those children who are already well on the way to becoming competent and fluent writers.

SECTION FIVE

HELPING CHILDREN BECOME BETTER SPELLERS

In this final section, let me draw together some of the main themes of the booklet, emphasising the practical aspects of what we can do to help children to become sound spellers and hence resourceful writers. I am conscious that the booklet may be addressing teachers who have a wide range of backgrounds. Certainly teaching emphases will vary both with the particular stage of education and with the skill and maturity of the pupils. For these reasons I propose to outline not one specific teaching approach but a range of principles and pointers for practice which can be taken up by different teachers and applied in a variety of ways.

Encouraging Pupil Autonomy

One of the principal themes to run through the booklet is that we need a clear idea of where we are heading as we seek to train children to spell and use words effectively. We can be helped in this by looking at the ways in which successful spellers operate, noting the range of strategies which they use and the flexibility which they develop to be able to handle different types of vocabulary in a wide variety of writing situations. Teaching emphases will vary with the age and maturity of the pupils, but the ultimate aim should be to provide all writers with the knowledge, skills and confidence to enable them (i) to spell individual words and use them effectively in writing, (ii) to proof-read their work to spot errors or to determine which words *may* be mis-spelled, and (iii) to know what to do, and where and how to refer, in order to make the necessary corrections.

The goal of spelling instruction is ultimately to do away with itself. Children who can be trained to learn about word structure from their reading and from routine experiences of handling words will need less time devoted to encouraging these activities. Writers who are learning to handle a range of types of information flexibly and simultaneously will eventually be in a position where they can be checking and modifying many of their spelling attempts as they are actually setting their ideas on paper. Most children, however, will need a substantial amount of guidance before they can reach this stage. They need a programme of training in the basic skills of handwriting and spelling, training in strategies for handling the processes of writing (planning, redrafting, proofreading) and systematic feedback from the teacher on various aspects of what they produce in order to help in the process of structuring the next piece of writing. The essential point is that there is still an important place in the education process for specific teaching of spelling, but that this is most valuable where it is part of a wider and ongoing language programme. There are two additional requirements for such a programme with respect to spelling. The first is that with respect to spelling it should encourage children in developing a working vocabulary whose function and meaning they understand. The second is that it should provide opportunities for tackling writing which stretches and develops the children's ability to think and reason, and which stimulates a confidence and desire to be involved in communicating particular messages *using writing*.

If studying spelling is assisted by a number of associated activities (for example, studying word structure and word use), so also autonomous spellers develop a wide range of associated strategies which they use to monitor their spelling performance in the course of their writing. Knowing when a word is spelled correctly is a help. Having a suspicion when it is wrong is also important, even if you are uncertain what the precise rendering should be. The more closely you can pinpoint letters which *may* be incorrect, the more quickly you can check your attempt against a model that is correct. Poorer spellers may need a lot of help with this, not just in learning to consult reference materials such as wordlists and dictionaries (primary teachers will be familiar with how much careful training some children require before they can isolate the information which they need in order to look up a word) but also in comparing the handwritten attempt with the type-written version to determine whether these are the same or different. Again, teacher support will be greatest in the early stages of learning, but even here the emphasis should be on developing skills of independence. The best materials are those which the child will eventually outgrow but which develop systematically the skills which are required for the next step.

Responding to Children's Writing

I stressed earlier that when children attempt to spell certain words they are testing their own hypotheses about how these words might be spelled in English. At some stage it will be important to receive feedback on the accuracy of these attempts, in order to learn from the experience of writing.

However, the question of how to respond to children's spelling in their writing is fraught with problems. Teacher feedback is more often negative than positive, focussing on the errors, not on the word which has at last been accurately spelled ('You've done it, John, you've spelled 'beautiful' correctly'). Comments on the speller, not the spelling, are particularly discouraging ('Do something about your spelling, Sharon') especially if the pupil is, in fact, making a real effort on a task which she finds genuinely perplexing.

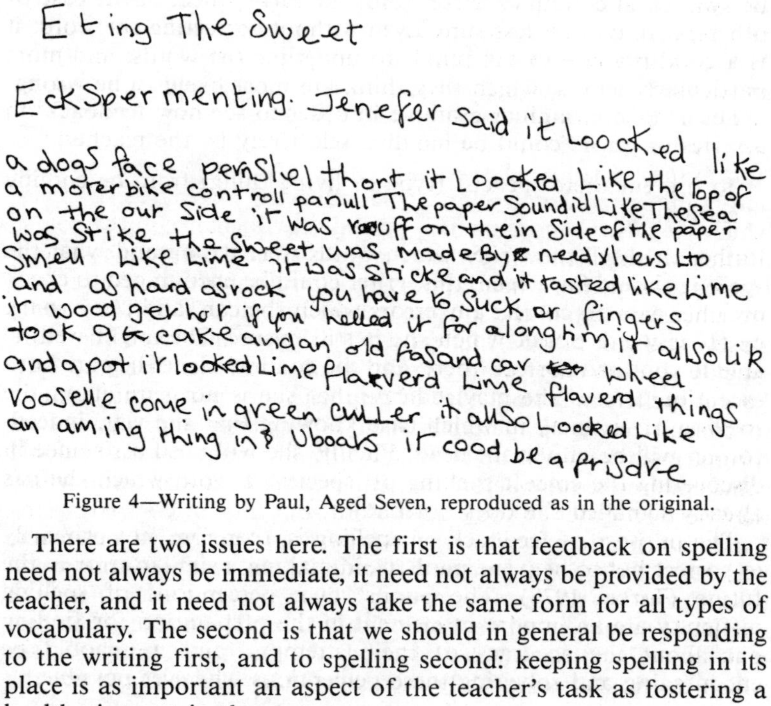

E t ing The Sweet

Eckspermenting. Jenefer said it Loocked like
a dogs face pernshel thort it Loocked Like the top of
a moterbike controll panull The paper Sound did Like The sea
on the our Side it Was ruuff on the in Side of the paper
was Strike the Sweet was made By needylers Lto
Smell Like Lime it was sticke and it tasted like Lime
and as hard as rock you have to Suck or fingers
it wood get hot if you helled it for a long him it allso lik
took a cake and an old fas and car wheel
and a pot it looked Lime flavverd Lime flaverd things
Vooselle come in green culler it allso Loocked Like
an aming thing in? Ubooks it cood be a priSdre

Figure 4—Writing by Paul, Aged Seven, reproduced as in the original.

There are two issues here. The first is that feedback on spelling need not always be immediate, it need not always be provided by the teacher, and it need not always take the same form for all types of vocabulary. The second is that we should in general be responding to the writing first, and to spelling second: keeping spelling in its place is as important an aspect of the teacher's task as fostering a healthy interest in the area.

Consider again Paul's writing on 'Eting the Sweet' (his spelling), reproduced in Figure 4 as in the original. What would you want to say to Paul about this piece of writing? What do you value in it? How do you think he could improve it if he were wanting to work on a new draft? How would you seek to discuss issues of handling and correction of spelling without in the process discouraging his freedom to select from a rich and varied vocabulary?

We have seen in earlier discussions that children can make a variety of kinds of errors when they are writing. Some will be execution errors, slips of the pen which occur because the writers are thinking about other things as they are recording the words, particularly where the task is complex. Essentially, these are words which the writer *does* know how to spell, and the mistakes will be easily detected when the work is re-read, when concern for content is no longer the main consideration. Other errors may be more genuinely the result of the pupil's lack of knowledge. Writers may be aware that certain of these words are mis-spelled; in the case of others, they may be less sure. Even without correcting the word, it is a good practice to ask pupils to underline the words, and more particularly letters, which they think are most likely to be wrong.

Let us take a familiar example in order to see how feedback on a series of errors could be handled selectively by the teacher:

To prevent there speacist (type of living thing) from be coming extinct.

Rather than tell the writer which words were wrong and what the spelling should have been, this writer could be encouraged to check over her answer, correct any errors which she can, and put a mark by those words about which she is still unsure. She might well be able to spot and correct 'there' and 'be coming' since they are both execution errors. She may indicate that she is not sure about the spelling of 'extinct', in which case knowing that she was, indeed, correct will be important news. Finally, she will need assistance in discovering the correct spelling of 'species', a word which she has already signalled she does not know.

The purpose of feedback on spelling is, therefore, not primarily to correct but to help the pupil avoid making a similar error in the future (Torbe, 1978). The pupils' own perceptions of spelling difficulty are an important element in the preparation for finding out about the accuracy of their attempts, and we should be encouraging and soliciting these perceptions wherever possible.

Pinpointing Vocabulary Needs

What kind of words should become the main focus for the specific study of spelling? Is there a common core vocabulary which all children need to master? To what extent do individuals differ in their vocabulary preferences and requirements, and to what extent are there differences across various ages and stages of development? These questions are important, not just in guiding pupils and teachers as they select specific words for studying, but also in suggesting which errors in a piece of writing the teacher most needs to bring to the pupil's attention.

We saw in Section Three that it can be helpful to consider how frequently certain words occur in children's writing: David learned the high-frequency words most quickly and efficiently, and he had more opportunities to use them again in his writing after they had been studied. However, not all high-frequency words (as drawn for a large corpus of children's writing) turned out to be high-frequency words for this particular pupil. We have seen, in addition, that different kinds of writing task can ask for specific types of vocabulary, even though they are not always so familiar to the individual. The *Alphabetical Spelling Lists* have now been revised in New Zealand to take account of some of these points and to allow teachers to make a wider range of judgements in selecting vocabulary for focussed work on spelling (Croft, 1983). The extensive surveys of children's writing in school which preceded the revision produced two findings of particular interest. Of almost 200,000 words which were surveyed, 75% could be covered by a list of only 300 items. This was the core vocabulary which was common to all the children, and even in different types of writing these same words recurred. By contrast, the remaining 25% of vocabulary which the children produced involved around 9,000 words and there was great variation across individuals. The researchers concluded:

'In effect, every child has a unique writing vocabulary. On the one hand, we have a relatively small common core of words that are used often. These can be adequately catered for in the spelling and word study segments of a sound classroom language programme. On the other hand, we have the diverse requirements of individuals writing about a potentially infinite set of topics. Catering for the development of this aspect of written vocabulary, and ensuring that accuracy of word-use and spelling keep pace with it, is the major challenge of every classroom spelling programme.'*

Addressing Spelling in the Primary School

So far many of the points which I have stressed apply equally to children in primary and secondary schools. Let me conclude by

* Croft, 1983, p11

highlighting a few of the issues which are more specific to the separate stages in the schooling system.

All children in primary school need to develop a clear method for studying the structure and spelling of new words. Some will acquire this with relative ease. Others will need careful instruction, with specific emphasis on relating the sequence of sounds to the visual pattern of the word, and training in writing from memory, not copying. The outcomes of this teaching need to be monitored, and various types of assessment may be used to evaluate aspects such as the child's particular strengths and weaknesses as a speller, the efficiency with which new words can be learned and recalled, the level of the child's spelling achievement in relation to his peers, the quality of the child's spelling in writing.* Parallel activities which encourage the study of word structure and word use, which promote vocabulary extension and which foster skills in proof-reading, checking, and use of reference materials are all related aspects of an on-going language programme which supports and develops the child's confidence and knowledge when handling words. Above all, children need opportunities to use their skills in writing. Where a reader for their script has been identified, there will be particular emphasis on achieving a version which is polished and finished. At other times, the writing may be largely for the child's own benefit, providing opportunities to 'explore, experiment and make errors' in order to acquire through practice the kind of confidence and fluency which can come only with use and experience.

There is an inherent advantage in the organisation of many primary and middle schools, since one specific teacher bears the overall responsibility for coordinating much of the pupil's curriculum. Not only does this help in tying the benefits from one activity to the next, but it also allows the teacher to introduce a wide range of activities even in pursuit of a single teaching goal. The important factor is that the teacher be able to establish an overall balance of emphasis. Thus with spelling, pupils can know that there will be times in the week when careful attention to accuracy is quite crucial, but others when it will be more important to focus on developing ideas or generating a rich and varied vocabulary. On certain occasions a polished piece of writing will be required from a single trial. At other times, pupils may have several opportunities to work on their scripts, developing and refining what they wish to say and how they wish to say it.

* Various examples of different approaches to assessment which cover these different aspects are given in Croft (1983).

So it is with spelling tuition. Provided that they are allowed neither to dominate nor to distort the general emphasis (which is that spelling is primarily a tool of writing), there are a wide number of word games and activities which can help children to develop flexible strategies for examining and handling words. Some examples are the use of mnemonics, games with prefixes and suffixes, play with nonsense words, study of the etiology of place names—these and many other suggestions can be found in several of the books listed in the bibliography.

I should stress that maturity as a writer is determined by ability and achievement in writing, not by age. Some children will attain a high level of skill in handling written language while they are still at primary school. If we continue the musical analogy, they are ready for the experience of performing and will find that the most significant lessons come when they are on the platform in front of an audience (even though the routine practising of scales will continue). These children are capable of writing with a genuine purpose for a real audience, and their writing will show most rapid development when they are given clear opportunities to do so.

Addressing Spelling in the Secondary School

The pupil's interest in how words are used and constructed, fostered by teachers in the primary school, need not stop with the transfer to secondary. Vocabulary demands increase considerably with the growing requirements of specific subjects to use specialised terms and, since learning about word use and spelling should go hand in hand, the proper setting for developing new vocabulary knowledge must be the individual classrooms of the different subject areas.

'We believe it (spelling) should be part of the fabric of normal classroom experience, neither dominating nor neglected.'

HMSO (1975), p 169.

So wrote the Bullock Committee in their document entitled, *A Language for Life*. If secondary pupils are to develop consistency in their approach to spelling and writing across the different subject areas of the curriculum, they will be helped if they can find a degree of consistency in the expectations and handling of spelling by different teachers whom they meet. Pupils can quickly become adept at attending to spelling only for the teachers who most specifically request it!

One of the main lessons to come out of Section Four is that

different writing tasks can place particular constraints on the writer. We need to understand these if we are to respond appropriately and sensitively to the pupils' efforts: circumstances of the writing (time pressure, opportunities for re-reading) can influence the efficiency with which even known words will be handled; specific tasks such as dictation create their own particular problems. Every script will not require an individual teacher response. For example, when all pupils require to use the same specific terms to complete, say, a worksheet or a passage of dictation, feedback can be handled predominantly as a whole-class activity. Tasks for the pupil which are more open-ended do, however, require responses from the teacher which are more highly individual.

The New Zealand approach identifies different kinds of vocabulary which can be studied in a variety of ways. A basic core vocabulary is so essential for daily writing that priority should be given to seeing that *all* children have mastered it as soon as they are able. For many this mastery will be attained in primary school. A specific priority for those who co-ordinate provision across the 10-14 age range should be to ensure that those who are still struggling in their attempts to establish this basic working vocabulary can be given additional opportunities, encouragement and support in the task. At least when they have this mastered, pupils will have the satisfaction of knowing that they can now tackle the majority of the words which they may need to use in writing!

Beyond this, the writing needs of different individuals will vary so widely that if specific study of words is still required it should be based on personal lists built up by the pupils from words which they have tried to use in writing but failed to use correctly. As have I already emphasised, the third type of vocabulary, that which is specific to a subject, is best handled in the course of general teaching in that area.

I wrote earlier of the importance of encouraging pupil autonomy in learning to spell. By adolescence, the twin issues of autonomy and motivation become critical. My own response with brighter secondary pupils who are still experiencing difficulty with spelling is to use direct teaching only for as long as it takes to demonstrate that they *can* improve in their ability to learn and remember new words. Thereafter, my role becomes one of facilitator, offering strategies to allow the pupils to become independent in their personal study of the vocabulary which they need to use in their day to day writing.

Since consistency across different subjects is important, questions are raised about who can coordinate developments in the secondary school. Certainly, there are likely to be a small number of pupils who will need continued support in learning to spell (as in a number of other areas) throughout their years of secondary schooling. Others may be coping successfully in most areas, but still have specific difficulties with spelling and writing. Yet others may be basically competent spellers, struggling only because they have not quite kept up with the vocabulary and other writing demands of each new subject.

Sometimes pupils may be extracted from the ordinary class for specific help. Even here, it is useful if the coordinating teacher can establish direct links with the work which is being set in the subject classes, not only to ensure the relevance of the help for the pupils but also to encourage a dialogue between different teachers. Subject teachers might be interested to see a portfolio of work collected across a number of subject areas, showing the range of work which particular pupils are capable of producing under a variety of circumstances.

Summary and Conclusions

If I had to take the lessons about spelling which we have considered in this booklet and reduce them to just one statement, it would be the following. The most important single factor in helping children to develop an interest in words and a care for how they are written is a corresponding care, interest and enthusiasm on the part of the teacher*. In addition, understanding something of the complexity of the spelling task and developing an appreciation of some of the constraints and pressures imposed by different types of writing can help teachers to become aware of the many achievements and frustrations which pupils experience as they write.

Children need to be given confidence to develop their own individual views. They also need the motive and the skills to be successful when they try to spell them out in writing.

* Peters (1970).

REFERENCES

ALBROW K (1974) The Nature of the Writing System and it Relation to Speech *in* WADE B and WEDDELL K (Eds) *Spelling: Task and Learner*, Educational Review Occasional Publications, No 5, University of Birmingham.

BARR J E (1983) *Spelling in the Context of Writing for a Purpose*, Unpublished PhD Thesis, Faculty of Education University of Birmingham.

BARR J E (in press) Spelling in Writing: Lessons from a Case Study, paper to be published in *Education* 3-13.

BARR J E and LAMBOURNE R D (1984) Analysing Spelling Performance on a Range of Purposeful Writing Tasks, *Educational Psychology*, 4, 197-311.

BEREITER C (1980) Development in Writing *in* GREGG L W and STEINBERG E R (Eds) *Cognitive Processes in Writing*, Hillsdale N J: Erlbaum.

BISSEX G L (1980) *Gnys at Work: A Child Learns to Read and Write*, Boston: Harvard University Press.

BRYANT P E and BRADLEY L (1980) Why Children Sometimes Write Words which they do not Read *in* FRITH U (Ed) *Cognitive Processes in Spelling*, London: Academic Press.

CLARK M M (1976) *Young Fluent Readers; What Can They Teach Us?* London: Heinemann.

CLARK M M, BARR J E and MCKEE F (1982) *Pupils with Learning Difficulties in the Secondary School: Progress and Problems in Developing a Whole-School Policy*, report of a Scottish Education Department funded project. Edinburgh: Scottish Council for Research in Education.

CROFT C (1983) *Spell-Write: an Aid to Writing, Spelling and Word Study*, Wellington: New Zealand Council for Education Research.

FERREIRO E and TEBEROSKY A (1983) *Literacy before Schooling*, London: Heinemann.

FRITH U (1983) The Similarities and Differences between Reading and Spelling Problems *in* RUTTER M (Ed) *Developmental Neuropsychiatry*, New York: Guildford Press.

FRITH U (1985) Cognitive Processes in Spelling and its Relevance to Spelling Reform *in* CLARK M M (Ed.) *New Directions in the Study of Reading*, Sussex: Falmer Press.

HMSO (1975) *A Language for Life*, Report of the Committee of Enquiry appointed under the Chairmanship of Sir Alan Bullock, Department of Education and Science.

HMSO (1980) *Learning and Teaching Primary 4 and Primary 7*, A Report by H.M. Inspectors of Schools, Scottish Education Department.

HOWARD E J (1971) *Something in Disguise*, London; Penguin.

LAMBOURNE R D and BARR J E (1984) Computer Analysis of Spelling and Vocabulary, *Educational Psychology*, 4, 313-320.

PAYTON S (1984) *Developing Awareness of Print: a young child's first steps towards literacy*, Educational Review Offset Publications, Faculty of Education, University of Birmingham.

PETERS M L (1970) *Success in Spelling*, Cambridge Monographs on Education, No 4, Cambridge Institute of Education.

PETERS M L (1985) *Spelling: Caught or Taught* (Revised Edition), London: Routledge and Kegan Paul.

SPENCER E (1983) *Writing Matters across the Curriculum*, Edinburgh: Scottish Council for Research in Education.

STERLING C M (1983) Spelling Errors in Context, *British Journal of Psychology*, 74, 353-364.

TORBE M (1978) *Teaching Spelling* (Second Edition), London: Ward Lock Educational.

WARD A (1867) *Artemus Ward in London, and Other Papers*, New York: Carleton & Co.

WHEATON (1977) *Alphabetical Spelling Lists*, Books One and Two. Exeter: Wheaton.

BIBLIOGRAPHY

SPELLING

General Background: the Nature of Skill in Spelling

ELLIS A W (1984) *Reading, Writing and Dyslexia: A Cognitive Analysis*, Hillsdale N J: Erlbaum.

FRITH U (Ed) (1980) *Cognitive Processes in Spelling*, London: Academic Press.

PETERS M L (1970) *Success in Spelling*, Cambridge: Cambridge Institute of Education.

PETERS M L (1985) *Spelling: Caught or Taught* (Revised Edition), London: Routledge and Kegan Paul.

WADE B and WEDELL K (Eds) (1974) *Spelling: Task and Learner*, Educational Review, Occasional Publications No. 5, University of Birmingham.

VALLING G H revised by SCRAGG D G (1965) *Spelling*, Deutsch.

Observations and Practical Advice on Teaching Spelling

ARVIDSON G L (1963) *Learning to Spell* (Manual to accompany the Alphabetical Spelling Lists), Exeter: Wheaton.

CROFT C (1983) *Teacher's Manual for Spell-Write*, Wellington: New Zealand Council for Educational Research.

LONGLEY C (Ed) (1975) *Adult Literacy Handbook*, London: BBC.

PETERS M L (1979) *Diagnostic and Remedial Spelling Manual* (Revised Edition), London: Macmillan.

POLLOCK J (1978) *Signposts to Spelling*, London: Heinemann.

TORBE M (1978) *Teaching Spelling* (Second Edition), London: Ward Lock Educational.

WESTWOOD P (1979) *Helping Children with Spelling Difficulties*, London: Macmillan.

Survey of Materials for Teaching Spelling

CRIPPS C and PETERS M L (in press) *Appraisal of Spelling Resources*, Centre for the Teaching of Reading, University of Reading.

WRITING

General Background: Writing Skills and the Nature of the Writing Task

APPLEBEE A N (1984) *Contexts for Learning to Write: Studies of Secondary School Instruction*, Norwood, N J: Ablex.

BRITTON J N, BURGESS A, MARTIN N, MICHAEL A and ROSEN H (1975) *Development of Writing Abilities, 11-18*, London: Macmillan.

CLARK M M and GLYNN T (Eds) (1980) *Reading and Writing for the Child with Difficulties*, Educational Review, Occasional Publications No. 8, University of Birmingham.

FERREIRO E and TEBEROSKY A (1983) *Literacy before Schooling*, London: Heinemann.

GRAVES D H (1983) *Writing: Teachers and Children at Work*, London: Heinemann.

GREGG L W and STEINBERG E R (Eds) (1980) *Cognitive Processes in Writing*, Hillsdale N J: Erlbaum.

KROLL B M and WELLS (Eds) (1983) *Explorations in the Development of Writing*, Wiley.

SMITH F (1982) *Writing and the Writer*, London: Heinemann.

WILKINSON A, BARNSLEY G, HANNA P and SWANN M (1980) *Assessing Language Development*, Oxford: Oxford University Press.

Observations and Practical Advice on Teaching Skills in Written Language

BYRNE D (1979) *Teaching Writing Skills*, London: Longman.

CCC: COMMITTEE ON PRIMARY EDUCATION (1982) *Hand in Your Writing*, Edinburgh: Committee on Primary Education.

DUNSBEE T and FORD T (1980) *Mark my Words*, Ward Lock Educational (in association with the National Association for the Teaching of English).

HARPIN W (1976) *The Second 'R': Writing Development in the Junior School*, London: Unwin Education Books.

HARRIS J and KAY S (1981) *Writing Development: Suggestions for a Policy 8-13*, Metropolitan of Rotherham: Education Department.

KRESS G (1982) *Learning to Write*, London: Routledge and Kegan Paul.

SCARDAMALIA M, BEREITER C and FILLION B (1981) *Writing for Results*, (Toronto: OISE; available in UK from The Scottish Council for Research in Education, Edinburgh).

SPENCER E (1982) *Writing Matters Across the Curriculum*, Edinburgh: Scottish Council for Research in Education.

THORNTON G (1980) *Teaching Writing: The Development of Written Language Skills*, Leeds: E J Arnold.